AN UNNECESSARY END

An Unnecessary End

A True Crime Story

Anonymous

TULLISIAN BOOKS
Publisher

Published by
Tullisian Books
PO Box 3118
Little Rock AR 72203-3118
http://tullisian.com

This is a work of non-fiction.

ISBN-13: 978-0-9979127-6-0 (Hardcover)

Library of Congress Control Number: 2022902327

ISBN-13: 978-0-9988855-0-6 (eBook)

ISBN-13: 978-0-9979127-4-6 (Kindle)

Date of Publication: 27 October 2022

Cover Design © Tullisian Books

TABLE OF CONTENTS

Publisher's Introduction

xcluding the COVID-19 pandemic's fatal mark on the world, approximately 150,000 people die each day around the world. The good news, if you wish to see it that way, is that two-thirds of deaths are age-related. That still leaves far too many untimely deaths caused by homicide, suicide, accidents, and other causes.

The purpose of this book is to heighten awareness of one particularly troubling cause of death. Many deaths, attributed to natural causes, are actually due to the deliberate actions of a caretaker. We usually are not made aware of this situation until a doctor or nurse is charged with multiple murders. If a doctor, nurse, family member, or other caretaker is responsible for only one or two deaths, they probably will get away with it. We should not allow that to happen.

The title selected for this book was inspired by a line from William Shakespeare's "Julius Caesar," Act II, Scene 2, "Seeing that death, a necessary end, will come when it will come."

An Unnecessary End

Death will come to all of us, but no one has the right to deliberately decide when some other person's death will happen.

This true story is being published unedited, in the author's own words.

AUTHOR'S INTRODUCTION

AN UNNECESSARY END

My story took place around a decade ago, but not a single day has gone by that I did not think about that time in my life.

This is not my first time to tell my story. At first, I chose not to tell anyone. I thought it would be better for everyone to believe the lie than to tell them a truth that I could not prove. I eventually decided to tell my two closest family members, my sister-in-law, and my nephew. They seemed unfazed by the truth. It was not the reaction that I expected to receive.

Some months later, I was at lunch with my ex-wife. I decided to tell her the story. Her reaction was similar to that of my relatives. To be honest, I want someone to be as outraged as I was.

Sometime later, I was visiting in the home of a lovely couple of friends. They have never met any of my family, but they have heard me talk about them. Our conversation covered both the lighthearted and the serious. I decided to tell them my story. They were shocked and appalled. It did make me feel a little better about my own strong feelings.

I have a lovely female friend out of state that I text with daily. One day we were texting about our families. I told her my story. Her only reply was "that would be very hard to prove." She is not wrong. Sadly, I cannot definitively prove what I know in my heart to be true. What you are reading, though, is the truth, the whole truth, and nothing but the truth.

The last person I told, before getting the opportunity to publish this book, was a male friend, also out-of-state, that I have known for many years. He simply replied with a story of his own.

His mother, in her early seventies, was admitted to a hospital for a non-life-threatening condition. That afternoon, a nurse approached my friend, introduced herself as his mother's nurse, and asked, "Do you want me to take care of her?"

He replied "Yes," assuming that all nurses take care of their patients.

His mother died that night.

There has never been any doubt in his mind who was responsible for his mother's death.

Since I began this book, the mother of one of my dearest friends passed away. She had hospice care at home and her death was imminent. However, a couple of months later, my friend told me that she was absolutely convinced that the hospice worker caused her mother's death.

None of these people have any knowledge of this book.

I am publishing this book anonymously because I want to bring awareness to this all-too-common occurrence. When people read my story, I want them to think, "This could be someone I know."

The true identity of the people in my story will be revealed at a later time.

Gentle readers, please do not judge this book for its literary merits. I am not pretending to compose The Great American Novel. I am simply telling my story, in my own words.

MY STORY

My Story

It was a perfectly ordinary, pleasantly busy, day at the office. The calmness of my day was shattered when my boss walked over to my desk and told me that my cousin was in the lobby to see me.

This was slightly disturbing for two reasons. One, no one has ever come to my office to see me. Two, I do not have a close relationship with any cousin. They would not even be aware that I had recently moved back to MediumCity from out-of-state, nor would they know where I was working.

I made my way to the elevator and down to the lobby as quickly as I could. Waiting for me was my nephew, my late brother's son. His being there was odd, so I knew that something bad had happened.

He had few details, but he knew that my mother, his grandmother, had a stroke and was in a hospital in SmallCity.

I returned to my office to inform my boss of the situation. My nephew and I were then on our way to SmallCity, a two-and-a-half-hour drive away.

It was a lovely November day, so we just enjoyed the ride. We had little knowledge of Mother's condition, so worrying about the unknown seemed a waste of time.

We arrived at the hospital and made our way to Mother's bedside. She had, indeed, suffered a stroke the previous night. My recently retired brother had been with her when it happened. She was first taken to the nearest hospital, a small one located in HomeTownAdjacent. They were not equipped to treat stroke patients and she was transferred to a large hospital in SmallCity, where we found her. She looked very tired, but otherwise normal. Fortunately, it was considered a mild stroke and the doctors expected no permanent physical or mental damage.

She remained at the hospital for a day or so and then returned to her house in HomeTown. My brother stayed with her for a while.

Traditionally, our parents hosted the entire family for holiday celebrations. After I moved back to

MediumCity, I took over the job of hosting. My father had been gone for several years and it was just too much work for Mother to handle. My apartment was too small for the number of family members and friends who showed up, but that seemed to make even more fun. At least we were all together.

We made it through Thanksgiving, Christmas, and Easter before everything changed. For our Easter dinner, my mother had asked about using her parents' dinnerware. She had given it to me more than twenty years before. I still had it packed away, so I did not bother with it. If I had known this was going to be our last big holiday at my apartment, I would certainly have unpacked those dishes. They are lovely. Her parents had received them as a wedding present.

It was another perfectly ordinary, pleasantly busy, April day at the office. Again, the calmness of my day was shattered when my boss told me that someone was in the lobby to see me. I knew that this was not going to be good news.

An Unnecessary End

It was my nephew again. Mother had suffered another stroke. She was once again in the large hospital in SmallCity, so off we went. Just like the last time, we had no details of her condition, so we just hoped for the best.

From what little I was told; it was the night of April fourteenth. Mother and Brother were sitting in side-by-side recliners, either sleeping or watching television, when she had the stroke. As it was happening, he told her, "This is the big one." I have no idea if she was able to understand what he was saying.

She was taken to the small hospital in HomeTownAdjacent, where they were still unable to do much for stroke patients. She was transported by ambulance to the large hospital in SmallCity. The way I see it, they knew that going to the small hospital would be a waste of time. She should have been taken to the large hospital immediately. Perhaps, then, any permanent damage could have been avoided.

By the time the doctor saw her in SmallCity, it was April fifteenth. He asked Mother if she knew what day it was.

"It is April fifteenth. Have you done your taxes?" she replied.

Apparently, he was amused by her response. He assured her that he had, indeed, filed his income tax and he commented that he thought she would be "just fine."

"Just fine" seems to be a stretch. She was paralyzed, probably forever, on the entire left side of her body. There was nothing that could be done about that.

Through two marriages, multiple other relationships, multiple residences, and multiple jobs, in MediumCity, Brother never really ever left our childhood home in HomeTown. Mother had even commented to me, not long after I moved back to MediumCity, that she wished Brother would just go home and leave her alone. She really did not want him hanging around her house all the time. Of course, she never told him that. But we are all happy that he was with her on that evening of April fourteenth. This would probably be a vastly different story if no one had been with her that night.

Being paralyzed, in any part of the body, is not something that anyone would want for themselves or a loved one. I had seen this before in my own family, so I knew that, under the right conditions, it could be manageable. It is not necessarily the end of the world.

I remember that day quite vividly. It was September or October in nineteen sixty-seven. Brother and I were both at football practice, which was just coming to an end for the day. Walking back from the football field to the locker room, I saw my mother sitting in her car. At the time, I was too busy to talk with her, but I certainly wondered why she was there.

She had come to get Brother, but not me. Without either of them saying anything to me, Brother got in the car, and they left. I finished up my work in the gym and walked home, still wondering what was going on.

It was getting dark outside, so when I opened the front door, the house seemed unusually dark. No one was at home.

My father and grandfather owned their own business, so the first thing I did was call there to find out what was going on. There was no answer.

I then called my grandparents' home. They should certainly be at home at this time of day. There was no answer there, either.

With no one else to call, I got busy with my normal afterschool chore, cleaning the kitchen. This was never a quick task. I had to handwash, dry, and put away the breakfast and lunch dishes, utensils, pots, and pans. At this point in her life, Mother had not yet picked up the habit of cleaning up as she went along, and we did not yet have a dishwasher. I also had to clean all the countertops, the stovetop, the kitchen table and chairs, and the floor.

Eventually, my parents and brother returned home. They had been at the hospital in HomeTownAdjacent. My grandfather had suffered a stroke. He was paralyzed on his left side.

An Unnecessary End

To this day, no one has ever been honest with me about why I was not told anything or allowed to go to the hospital. To be honest, I honestly believe that Mother did not want to come home to a dirty kitchen. Since Brother did not have daily chores to do, he could go to the hospital without affecting anything or anyone. If I had gone to the hospital, the kitchen would still be a mess. Not having chores was one of Brother's benefits of being the favorite son.

My grandfather was only sixty-three when he had the stroke, much younger than Mother was. He was also in better general health than she was, but from the beginning, I had hopes that she would come through it as well as he had.

There was, of course, a transition period, but my grandfather eventually was quite able to get around on his own. He had my grandmother there to assist, but with the help of a crutch, he was able to walk around the house. With an electric wheelchair, he was even able to get out of the house and drive it on the streets of HomeTown.

He lived for nine years before succumbing to a heart attack.

After a few days in the hospital, Mother was discharged and allowed to go home, with plans for Brother to stay with her.

After one night – just one night - Brother told her that he could not deal with her situation, and he moved her to a nursing home in HomeTownAdjacent. One thing that he had always promised her was she would never have to live in a nursing home.

Sister-in-law, Nephew, and I were all working full time, but we drove down on Saturday to visit with Mother at the nursing home. The home seemed quite nice, and she seemed perfectly happy there. She already knew some of the other residents, so that helped. She received mandatory physical therapy, which I was happy about. We made it down to visit her for two Saturdays in a row before everything changed again.

For reasons that were never made perfectly clear to me, Mother was transferred to a large hospital in

MediumCity. If she had to be in a hospital, I was happy with this one. It is only about two miles from my apartment, so I was able to spend as much time as possible with her.

It was during this hospital stay that I began to see a different side of Brother.

There were many conversations about where Mother would go when she was discharged from this hospital. The two options were her house in HomeTown or my apartment in MediumCity. I only had a one-bedroom apartment, but there was enough space in the living room to put her hospital bed. Her own house seemed like the obvious choice, but she initially chose to stay at my apartment. It seems that the ambulance ride from the nursing home to the hospital in MediumCity had been quite uncomfortable, painful even. She dreaded having to make such a long ambulance ride again. As soon as it was explained to her that she would be given enough Morphine to make her comfortable, she was sold on the idea of going home to her own house and friends.

By this point in her recovery, we also knew that I would take a leave of absence from my job to take care of Mother. FMLA (Family and Medical Leave Act) would give me three months away from my job. Brother did his best to convince me that Mother would not live even that long.

Every time I made a comment or asked a question about her condition or her future care, Brother's standard reply was "She is just going home to die." I cannot even begin to tell you how many times I heard him say that. "She is just going home to die" was his answer to everything.

On three occasions during her hospital stay, Brother and I met with a lovely woman at the hospital to discuss Mother's ongoing physical therapy. She was so wonderful and gave us so much of her time and expertise. It was a day or so after our third meeting that I asked Brother a question about the plans for physical therapy. He looked at me like I was crazy and said something like, "She is not ever going to have physical therapy. She is just going home to die."

I do not remember how many days she spent at the hospital, but it was finally time for her to go home. The big day would be on Monday, the day after Mother's Day.

Brother had gone on to HomeTown to be there on Monday morning when a hospital bed was to be delivered. I was at the hospital to see Mother off. Two particularly good friends, a mother and daughter, also came to see her off. Their presence was a wonderful surprise.

The two ambulance men seemed extremely nice and caring. Mother was in good hands for the long ride home.

After I saw the ambulance pull away, I drove home and packed my clothes and a few essentials, including my two cats, and made my return to HomeTown. I had no idea what was to come.

By the time I made it to HomeTown, Mother was happily in her own home, after being away almost a month, and comfortably settled in her new hospital bed.

Immediately before leaving the hospital, one of Mother's doctors gave me instructions regarding one of her prescriptions. One of the first things I told Brother after I arrived in HomeTown was the message from her doctor. Brother gave me that "you stupid fool" look and told me that we were not going to give Mother any medicine. I expected him to remind me for the zillionth time that "she had only come home to die," but I do not remember him saying it at that time. Maybe he held back because Mother was only a few feet away.

I also knew that "no medicine" did not include Morphine or Tylenol PM, which we would give Mother as needed for pain.

It became crystal clear almost immediately that I would be Mother's primary caregiver. Brother would take a secondary role. I would also be primarily responsible for housekeeping, meals, laundry, and the household bank account. The only job I would not have to worry about was lawncare. With over an acre to mow, Mother already had people hired to take care of the yard.

This situation was not new to me. I grew up in a "Cinderfella" house. I did not have two stepsisters, but I did have two older brothers. I was not raised the same way they were.

I have "joked" my entire life that the only reason I was born was because Mother wanted a live-in maid. In one convenient package, she got a housekeeper, groundskeeper, go-fer, personal assistant, and dresser.

I did it all without question, except for one morning. We were getting ready for school when Mother told me to make up Brother's bed. I had already made up my own bed. I questioned her on it and her reply was, "You do a lot better job than he does." I did not respond, but if I had, I would have suggested that she teach him how to do a good job.

Can you guess who said "thank you" after I made up his bed? No one!

If there is an upside to the way things were growing up, it is that I learned to be an adult at an incredibly young age.

As a result of the way I grew up, I had no problem with whatever was expected of me. I was accustomed to working, so taking care of Mother was my new full-time job, for as long as necessary.

Our biggest assistance came to us the next day when "Honey" began working with us. She was our hospice worker, an employee of the state. We did not meet each other in advance. Her first day of the job was our first meeting, but we could not have asked for a better fit. She was authorized to work only two hours a day, Monday through Friday, so we hired her to stay an extra two hours each day. She even came by on some Saturdays and Sundays. This gave me time to go grocery shopping or run other errands without having to leave Mother alone in the house, something we never did.

My decision to call her Honey for this story is a little backward. After she had been coming every day for a while, she began the habit of yelling "Honey, I'm home" in a sing-songy way as she got out of her car. She always made herself laugh. The name Honey always makes me think of that.

It took us all almost no time at all to get into a regular routine. It may sound monotonous, but I did not find it that way. I tend to like a regular routine. Every morning, Honey bathed her, changed her gown, and changed the sheets on her bed. Every day, I then had laundry to do. As needed, there were shampoos, manicures, and pedicures. Some days Mother had breakfast before all of this happened. Some days it was after. I do not want to sound unkind, but taking care of Mother, who was completely bedridden, was like taking care of a baby – who could talk!

There were two things that were done at the hospital that we continued doing at her house. One was giving her regular small doses of Morphine. The other was hand feeding her. It did not take long before I knew we needed to make a couple of changes.

AN UNNECESSARY END

Mother's bedroom was an exceptionally large room that had an outside door to a patio. There is a glass storm door in addition to the wood door. The wood door was kept open during the day, for the most part, and Mother could see across the patio and down the street. She began telling us about things that she could see outside. None of what she talked about was really out there, but we could not convince her otherwise. She also told us about the horrible nightmares she was having. I knew that all of these nightmares and hallucinations had to be caused by the Morphine, so we stopped giving her those regular doses. The nightmares and hallucinations stopped immediately. We still kept Morphine on hand but gave her small doses only when she needed it. One problem solved.

The other thing that bothered me was hand feeding her all the time. Granted, she did not actually ask us to hand feed her, but that is something that they did at the hospital. She was right-handed. It was her left side that

29

was paralyzed. Why could she not feed herself? It turned out that she could. Unless it was to cut up her food, she did not need help at all.

I still had hope that she would someday become as mobile and self-sufficient as my grandfather had. As time went on, I knew that it was not going to happen. That is okay, though. We will just make the best of the situation that we were given.

I do not know why this did not occur to me right from the very beginning, but as you will find out, sometimes it takes me a while to see all the pieces of the puzzle, let alone put them all together.

Mother's entire world consisted of her bed and its immediate surroundings. I needed to do anything that I could to make this small corner of the world as nice for her as possible.

Over a period of months, I continued to buy beautiful, and colorful, sheet sets. I bought her a series of gowns, trying to coordinate them with the color of the sheets. I also bought bottle after bottle of nail polish. I really think doing this actually did brighten her spirits. It even brightened Honey's spirits. She was always excited when she saw my most recent purchases.

Right from the start, it was not necessary for both Brother and I to be there. Although there were many times that we were both in HomeTown, he began spending more time at his own apartment in MediumCity. I usually made to trip to MediumCity once a week myself to check on my own apartment, pick up mail, etc. Brother was always there to take care of Mother in my absence. Like I said earlier, we had a regular routine and it worked for us.

Mother usually had visitors every day, most often in the afternoons. For all but one of us, this was usually a highlight of the day. Brother never wanted to see or talk to any of the people who came over. Once, a lady with whom he had gone to school, and her mother came by to visit. They were actually two of Mother's most frequent visitors. Brother was in the living room. Mother asked me to get him so that he could say hello. I did, not thinking it would be any big deal.

"Tell them I'm not here," he said, obviously very irritated.

"They know you are here," I said.

He stormed off, through the living room, through the dining room, and down the hall to Mother's bedroom. He was livid. As soon as he reached the bedroom door, the fake smile came out, the fake enthusiasm came out, and he acted like seeing them was the best thing that had happened to him in a long time.

At that moment, it dawned on me that what I had just seen was Brother in a nutshell. He will say anything, no matter how awful, behind someone's back. To their face, though, he is their best friend in the world. He does it to family members, friends, co-workers, everyone. I have seen it so often, but most people only get to see the happy face-to-face part. They never know what he really thinks of them. They would be shocked if they knew what he had probably said about them behind their backs. Brother always wants people to think he is such a wonderful person.

Mother had visitors practically every day, usually in the afternoons. I really enjoyed these visits, probably as much as Mother did. Some, like the mother and daughter I mentioned earlier, as well as the pastor at Mother's church, were there pretty much every week, maybe even more than once. Others made regular, but more sporadic, visits.

Most of the visitors were people I had known my entire life. I just had not seen some of them for forty-plus years. Others were new acquaintances. Regardless of how long I had known them, I just thought it was so lovely that they cared enough about my mother to spend time with her.

My nephew and sister-in-law drove down from MediumCity every Saturday to visit with us. No one expected them to make such frequent visits, it is a five-hour round trip after all, but it was certainly appreciated. We always had a good day with them.

An Unnecessary End

I have learned from personal experience, both from my time with Mother and also from my own time in the hospital several years later, that you just cannot predict who will come for a visit. Some of the people that you truly expect to be there for you just never show up. Other people, those that you never dreamed would bother to show up, surprise you with multiple visits. People will definitely surprise you.

Even though I have written about how much my mother enjoyed being pampered, she was in no way, a lazy person. Quite the opposite, in fact. She was quite the worker. She did not retire until she was in her early eighties, just about a year or so before her stroke.

She always had multiple careers going on simultaneously. One of them, for a global cosmetics company, lasted more than fifty years. She began it when I was only five years old. She only gave it up when the stroke prevented her from continuing. If not for the stroke, she probably would have stayed with them until the day she died.

An Unnecessary End

A few days after we returned to HomeTown, Mother received a letter from the cosmetics company. I did not read it, but she told me that it, quite curtly, told her that because she had not placed an order for the past three campaigns, she was no longer associated with the company. After devoting more than half a century to this company, she was devastated, and I do not blame her for feeling so upset. When she received the letter, she actually thought it might be a thank you for her decades of success with the company. It was quite the opposite.

I saw how hurt she was by this so, without her knowledge, I wrote a letter to the CEO. I described Mother's fifty-plus years of service to the company, and I informed her of Mother's health condition. The only thing I asked for was a letter to Mother acknowledging and thanking her for her dedication to the company.

There was no reply within what I thought was a reasonable length of time. Giving her the benefit of the doubt, mail does get lost sometimes, I sent the CEO a copy of my letter.

No one at that company ever bothered to respond to my letters. People can really let you down sometimes.

That CEO was later removed from the company.

All aspects of our new normal life continued, but as August approached, some deadlines loomed over us. My ninety-day FMLA leave from work would end in August. The daily hospice care was originally set up for only ninety days. It would end in August, also. Then what would we do?

Brother's hateful and repeated comments that Mother had only come home to die proved to be only wishful thinking on his part.

Things usually have a way of working out, though. It was apparent that I would not return to work, so I submitted my letter of resignation. I did not hate doing that as much as I thought I would. The hospice agency, my biggest concern, assured me that they would be with us for as long as necessary. That was a huge relief. August came and went without any changes to our routine.

My intimate knowledge of stroke victims is limited to the two people I have already mentioned, my paternal grandfather and my mother. However, I am going to go out on a limb and say that, just like snowflakes, no two strokes are alike.

Even though he died in nineteen seventy-six, I have very vivid memories of my grandfather. When he would sit down, either in the living room or at the dining table, he would use his good right hand to gently place his paralyzed left hand in his lap, carefully straightening his fingers. I do not think he was even aware that he was doing it, but I would often see him touch and softly stroke his left hand. He touched it in a way that you would, or should, touch a lover.

One afternoon, I commented to Mother that I had never seen her touch her left hand. Her left arm was always to the side, resting on the bed. I asked her if she could place her left hand on top of her stomach. She felt around for quite a while, but she could never find her left hand. I then placed her left hand on top of her stomach and asked her to touch it. Again, she felt around for quite a while, but she never found it. I asked her to look down so that she could see her left hand, and then touch it. She said that she could not see it.

For some remarkable reason that I may never understand, her brain would simply not let her acknowledge that she still had her left arm and hand.

I think Mother had always accepted the fact that this is the way her body would remain for the rest of her life. Occasionally, though, she would tell me that she genuinely believed that one morning she would wake up and be able to walk again. Without saying that I did not think that would ever happen, I did tell her that even if the paralysis went away, she would still require physical therapy before she could walk again. I never could get her to understand why, though. Thinking about it now, though, it would have taken an absolute miracle for the paralysis to go away. If that miracle happened, I guess another miracle could have happened that would give her the ability to walk again. It did not matter anyway. The paralysis never got any better.

December twenty-third was a special day. It was Mother's eighty-fourth birthday. I had put all of the Christmas decorations in Mother's bedroom, so there was already a festive feel to the room. She was surprised when people began showing up for her birthday party that morning. Honey was already there, of course. Nurses from the hospice agency came, as well as her pastor. There was cake, balloons, and gifts. It was a nice party for what would be her final birthday.

That evening, a large group of Christmas carolers came by. A group from Mother's church and a group from another church saw each other caroling and joined together in one big group. Fortunately, there was enough space in Mother's bedroom for all of them to come in. They sang quite a few traditional Christmas carols and then surprised

Mother - and me - with a big finale of "Happy Birthday."

Did you notice who did not bother to show up for Mother's birthday? There was no sign of Brother that day.

Now it is time to move on to March, the beginning of the end.

One day, toward the end of March, I think, Brother told me that he wanted me to withdraw money from one of Mother's Certificates of Deposit and put the money in the household account. I did question this because I knew that there was no immediate need to do this. I had been handling the household finances for ten months and I knew that there was plenty of money there for the foreseeable future.

Brother explained that he wanted the extra money there in case Mother passed away. He wanted it to pay for her funeral.

I had no reason to believe that Mother was going to pass away soon. She was doing as well as, or probably better than, she was when she came home from the hospital. She was feeling well, eating well, and sleeping well. She was enjoying her friends' visits. She was still enjoying her life and she did not hesitate to let everyone know that she was not ready to leave this Earth.

As you know by now, as I have always known, life is so much better when Brother gets his way. I transferred the money just as he wanted.

It did not occur to me until I was writing this that I had to transfer the money from an account with my name on it to an account with his name on it. I had just transferred part of my inheritance to him. I am sure that he was well aware of this at the time.

Fast forward a week or two to the early part of April.

It had been an ordinary day, nothing memorable, except that it was one of the infrequent nights when Brother and I were both in HomeTown. On those occasions, Brother always slept in the room with Mother because he preferred to sleep in a recliner than in a bed. I slept on the floor in Mother's room when Brother was not there.

AN UNNECESSARY END

At around ten o'clock that evening, I was ready to go to bed. I went back to say goodnight to Mother. She was still awake, but ready for a good night's sleep herself. I gave her a hug and a kiss on the forehead, I believe, and went to my bedroom.

The following morning, I awoke to what I assumed would be a normal day. I showered and dressed, ready for Honey's arrival.

Brother was in the kitchen, so I decided to speak with him before going back to say good morning to Mother. He told me that Mother was still sleeping and that he did not want anyone to disturb her. He said he wanted her to sleep as long as she could. He had even called Honey to tell her not to come in that day.

Of course, everything about that seemed odd, but it was Brother, so what else could I expect? I do not think I even made a comment. I just left the room.

Think about this for a moment. Mother was confined to bed for every minute of every day. If there was anyone on Earth getting all the sleep they needed, it was her. With only one exception that I can remember, Mother was always awake before Honey arrived each morning at nine o'clock.

I then went back to Mother's room to check on her myself. She appeared to be fine. She seemed to be sleeping.

A short time later, the pastor, one of Mother's most frequent guests, stopped by for a visit. I greeted him on the patio just outside Mother's bedroom. As I have said before, Brother never had any interaction with Mother's guests, at least not by choice. Today, though, he quickly joined pastor and I on the patio. He immediately informed the pastor that Mother was sleeping and that he did not want anyone to disturb her. The pastor then said that he just wanted to peek in on her. Brother emphatically told him no. Maybe I should have interfered, but I just stayed out of it.

I had never before seen the pastor show any signs of anger, but he was clearly angry with Brother. He left, though, without an argument.

An Unnecessary End

It soon became clear that Mother was not simply sleeping, but even when the pastor returned that afternoon, Brother refused to let him in the house. Again, his anger was quite apparent.

I do not think that any other people stopped by that day. If they did, Brother stopped them before I even knew they were there.

As truly bizarre as I thought it was that someone could be perfectly fine at ten o'clock at night and in a coma the next morning, I remembered that I had seen this exact thing happen once before. It calmed my brain a little by thinking, "It is okay. These things do happen."

The next few days were back to our normal routine. Honey came every day. Some visitors still came to check in on her, but I think the word had gotten out and most people stayed away. Anyone who asked about her, though, I still encouraged them to come by and see her and talk to her.

I do not mean to be indelicate, but Mother did develop bad breath while she was in a coma. I do not know how hospitals deal with dental hygiene for coma patients, but I did the only thing that I thought I could. Brushing her teeth and rinsing with mouthwash did not seem possible, so I poured some mouthwash on a paper towel and wiped down her teeth, gums, and tongue. To my surprise, she did not like that at all. I was not expecting any reaction from her, but she fought back. She moved her head around trying to get me to stop. She did not say any words, but she made plenty of noise to let me know she was not enjoying that. I finished as quickly as I could, and I never tried that again.

On one of her coma days, Brother informed me that I needed to go to the funeral home and start making plans for her funeral. People do come out of comas, but I just had a feeling that we would not be so fortunate.

He let me know, in no uncertain terms, that he would have nothing to do with making funeral arrangements, other than to say that it would have to be a closed casket service. He was emphatic that he would never look at her after she died.

We already knew that it would be a simple graveside service. I knew that she wanted a casket just like the one that she selected for my father, and I knew that she was to be buried in the same grave with my father. I did not even know that was a thing, but my father's grave had been dug deeper than normal to accommodate her casket on top of his.

After I left the funeral home, I went to the florist across the street to select the family arrangement that would be on top of the casket. I ordered a variety of flowers all in shades of pink and purple.

As much as I hoped that Mother would wake up from her coma, and still believed that there was that real possibility, all hope disappeared on the morning of Tuesday, April twelfth.

The day began no differently than any of the other past few days. Even before it was time for Honey's arrival, our assigned social worker dropped by for a visit. She always visited with Mother, but her primary focus was supposed to be on Brother and me. Of course, since Brother did not like to talk with anyone who visited, it was always I who spoke with her.

When Honey arrived, I was still occupied with the social worker, talking on the patio. Therefore, Brother went with Honey to begin Mother's daily routine. Only a minute or two passed before they both came running out of house, not knowing what had happened with Mother.

I ran inside to see what had startled them so. I must admit, I was quite startled and confused myself. Without doing anything to Mother, I called and asked for a nurse to come by.

I do not remember if the social worker went into Mother's bedroom, but she was gone by the time the nurse arrived.

We were familiar, after a year's time, with all of the nurses who were assigned to us. They all took turns making regular visits to check on Mother. The nurse who arrived was one that we knew well.

Since I was now available, Brother went about his business and left Honey and I to deal with Mother.

Having been a nurse for many years, she knew immediately when she saw Mother that she had bled out. I had certainly heard of that happening, but I had never seen it myself. It is quite unnerving.

Honey and I began helping the nurse, who was so calm about everything, get Mother cleaned up. After just a couple of minutes, it all just seemed to hit me at once. I was still doing my part, but tears were flowing quite freely down my face. Honey saw me and began crying, also. It became too much for her and she ran outside, leaving the nurse and I to finish up.

I was actually quite thankful for the nurse's calm and peaceful demeanor. I could not have gotten through that, otherwise.

The remainder of the morning and the entire afternoon were quite peaceful. Even after bleeding out, Mother continued to breathe normally, but we all knew now that it was just a matter of time. The end would come soon.

During my year in HomeTown, I tried to participate with the community the best that I could, given my limited free time. I attended funerals. I went to our neighbor's ninetieth birthday party. I did as much business with local merchants as I could, but that was not terribly easy. In the decades since I had moved away from HomeTown, the population of the town had doubled, but the number of businesses was down more than half.

I had heard that one of the surrounding rural volunteer fire departments was having a dinner to raise money for the department. I did not think that I would know any of the people involved, but I wanted to do my small part to help out. Plus, it would keep me from having to fix dinner that evening.

Before I left, I checked on Mother to see how she was doing. There had been no change since that morning, but I knew that I could not be away for long.

I only had to drive a few miles out of town. When I arrived, I was pleasantly surprised. It was not quite time for serving to begin and the place was packed. They had one long line for all orders, dine in and to go, so I took my place in line. To my surprise, I actually saw someone I knew, a woman that I had attended first through twelfth grades with. I had not seen her since nineteen seventy-one, and she still looked the same. We had a lovely visit.

As soon as I received my two orders, one for Brother and one for me, I hurried home as quickly as possible.

I ran in through the kitchen door, placed the bag of food on the kitchen table, and made my way to Mother's bedside. Brother was in the room with her, but he had fallen asleep watching television and was not paying any attention to her.

I leaned against the rails of her hospital bed and silently watched her face. She was now breathing extremely slowly. I just continued to watch her, focusing on her breathing. At one point, there had been so much time since her last breath, that I told Brother that I thought she was gone. He got out of his recliner and came over. Mother then took another breath. Within a few minutes, though, her breathing did stop for good. Mother was gone.

We had been instructed that, when the time came, the only call we needed to make was to the hospice agency. They would make all necessary calls and send a nurse to the house. I called the agency as I was told to do.

Brother, on the other hand, immediately began making calls. In addition to friends and family, he called the coroner's office. In fact, I am not really sure who all he called.

There was one call that he made that really bothered me. The hospice agency had arranged for the hospital bed to be delivered to us. It was also the hospice agency who would be responsible for having the bed picked up. Brother was so anxious to have the bed, and all traces of Mother, removed that he called and demanded that they pick it up on Wednesday, the day after Mother died.

In less than twenty-four hours after her death, Brother had her bedroom looking like she had never been there.

Going back to that Tuesday evening, the on-call nurse happened to be one that we had never met. She called to say that she lived about an hour away and would be there was quickly as she could. This gave me a chance to get Mother's clothes ready. I should have been more prepared, but I was not. I knew what clothes Mother wanted to be buried in. They were hanging in her closet. Since Mother had not worn clothes for the past year, I wanted to wash them, so that they would be nice and fresh. Luckily, I had time to do so.

The nurse was actually the first person to arrive. I had never met this young woman before, and she was extremely sweet. I do not know if it was something she said or exactly what happened to me, but I almost immediately broke down in front of her.

She held me tight and let me cry on her shoulder.

My odd brother chimed in with something like, "I did not think he would care," talking about me as if I were not even in the room. The nurse and I both ignored him.

It was only a short while later that the room was filled with all the necessary people required to deal with a death.

Obviously, these people were not familiar with Mother's story, so one man began asking Brother and I questions about Mother's cause of death. We explained to him the stroke last year and the coma last week and that her death was simply a result of all of that.

At the time, and for quite some time later, I honestly believed that Mother had died due to complications of a stroke. Only Brother knew the truth about what had happened last week, and he had no problem lying about it.

How much Morphine had he given her? How did he get her to drink it? I assume that he simply poured it into whatever she was sipping on at the time. He probably had to encourage her to drink it all before going to sleep.

On Wednesday, I went to the funeral home to see Mother and give my final approval on what they had done and to put her wedding ring on her finger. Not surprisingly, seeing her brought me to tears, but I did try to control my emotions in front of the funeral home employee. I did not expect anything to be unsatisfactory, and I was certainly not disappointed. Mother looked beautiful. The casket was exactly what I had ordered. The flowers were stunning. The florist had done an outstanding job.

Out of all the sheet sets that I had purchased for Mother, there was one set that was the favorite of all three of us, Mother, Honey, and me. Brother would never even be aware of such things. It had a white background with stylized flowers. The pillowcases were solid lavender. Out of all the nail polish that I had purchased, there was one that was our favorite. It was a shade of lavender.

When Mother passed away, it just so happened that her favorite sheets were on the bed, which the funeral home employees wrapped her in, and she was wearing her favorite nail polish.

I later found a woman online who makes stuffed bears out of the clothing, or other fabric, of someone who has passed away. I sent her the flat sheet and pillowcase, and she made me two stuffed bears to have as a keepsake.

Later in life, Mother had gotten a new wedding ring. It was, shall we say, more impressive than her original wedding ring. I now have her newer ring and wear it often. But she wanted to be buried with her original ring. It was a lovely ring, also. It was a narrow yellow gold band with a single row of five small diamonds. That ring was "meant to be" because it eventually represented our family of five – mother, father, and three sons. I placed it on her perfectly manicured, with lavender polish, ring finger.

I left the funeral home pleased with everything that they had done. Visitors, and there were many, could now pay Mother a visit.

I scheduled the family visitation at the funeral home for Thursday evening. My sister-in-law and nephew drove down from MediumCity to be there. It was just the three of us. Brother refused to be there. He stayed at home and watched television.

There was a lovely turnout of family and friends. Mother would have been pleased that so many people came to pay their respects.

The funeral, a lovely graveside service, took place on Friday morning, April fifteenth, exactly one year to the day after Mother had been admitted to the hospital in SmallCity following her stroke. As Brother demanded, the casket was closed. He never saw Mother after she was taken from our house.

We were already having warm Spring days, but on the day of her funeral, it was quite cool – sweater or jacket weather for most people. There was some significance in that, I felt. I do not know why.

An Unnecessary End

As there had been the night before, there was a lovely turnout for her funeral. The only speaker was her pastor, who had been so kind to us for the past year. He was certainly one of Mother's most loyal and frequent visitors. We could not have appreciated him more.

I somehow managed to hold it all together throughout the service – until the very end. The pastor concluded the service by asking everyone to join in song. Sometimes we just have no control over our emotions. I dropped my head and cried.

After the song, Brother, dressed in his Hawaiian shirt (well, it did have a black background), jumped to the front and thanked everyone for coming. He said it the same way he would if he was thanking people for coming to his birthday party.

Looking back now, all of the suspicious details were there in plain sight. Why did it take me so long to realize that Brother had carefully planned and conducted his murder scheme? It is difficult to believe that your own brother would, without remorse, give your mother a fatal dose of Morphine. He was probably upset that she did not die immediately, but he still got what he wanted.

The question of why is always there in cases like this. What was his motive? His primary motive was that he simply did not want to deal with her anymore. He wanted her out of his life. Brother always finds a way to remove situations and people that he no longer wants in his life. The other motive was money. It is always about money, isn't it? Brother did not need her money but want and need are two entirely different things. Our nephew and I each inherited approximately one-third of her money. Brother inherited the remainder of her money, along with her house, all of its furnishings, and her vehicle. It does pay to be the favorite son.

FINAL THOUGHTS

An Unnecessary End

n the previous chapter, I wrote about how surprised (shocked, actually) I was when Mother went into a coma so suddenly and for no obvious medical reason. I also wrote that I had seen this situation one time before. That is the only thing that made this situation at all believable or acceptable.

The following is the story of that first time. I will bet that you can easily figure out the common denominator in these two situations.

When I first moved back home to MediumCity, I stayed for the first month with my brother – until I could find a suitable place of my own. It was within walking distance of my new job, which was great because I was without a car at that time.

One afternoon, when I left the office, I decided to walk to a nearby fast-food restaurant for dinner. At around the halfway point on my walk back to my brother's apartment, a red car, which I had never seen, pulled up beside me. It was my brother and his first ex-wife, whom I will call XSIL (ex-sister-in-law).

This was my first time seeing her since I had moved back.

Brother was driving XSIL's car and as soon as he parked the car, he jumped out of the car to take (or make) a cellphone call. He seemed very agitated and angry about something.

I sat down in the driver's seat to visit with XSIL.

XSIL has been plagued with health problems for almost her entire life. It began in her early-to-mid teens when she was diagnosed with rheumatoid arthritis. I have never known anyone else who has had as many health problems as XSIL, but she has faced them all with grace and a smile. I am sure that she has had many dark moments, but she never let them show.

Her most recent battle was with cancer, but she fought hard and came through a winner. During the course of our lively conversation, she asked if I wanted to feel her hair. I know that there are many people who always want to touch a pregnant woman's belly or touch the short buzzcut of a cancer survivor.

Although I would call myself a touchy-feely person, I am not one to ask someone if I can touch them. XSIL insisted and I ran my fingers through her short hair. It felt lush and strong. To me, it was a sure sign that she was getting better.

We finished our conversation, and I got out of the car. Brother got in and they drove away. Brother and I never really spoke with each other that afternoon.

I really enjoyed my visit with XSIL and, now that I was once again living in MediumCity, I looked forward to spending more time with her, making up for all those years that I was away.

XSIL had a primary caregiver, a hired aid who was with her during the day. Brother acted as her secondary caregiver and usually checked on her every late afternoon or early evening.

As I recall, it was only a couple of days after my visit with XSIL that Brother told me that she was in a coma. That did not make sense to me. How could that happen? I had just seen her, and she was feeling so very well. She had seemed so happy and full of life.

For the next two evenings, I went with Brother to XSIL's house. Her daytime caregiver had been with her, but when we arrived, no one else was in the house. XSIL was lying in bed, looking as if she had been laid out in a coffin.

I had absolutely no say in her care, but I did have a lot of questions – which I kept to myself. Why was she not in a hospital where she could be monitored 24/7? Why is she not getting any nutrition? What if she wakes up when no one is there?

My questions never went away, but they soon became irrelevant. Within days of going into a coma, XSIL passed away.

With her lifelong health problems, XSIL always knew that she should be prepared. She had written her own obituary and planned her own memorial service well in advance.

Her obituary was pretty straightforward. There were no real surprises. But for me, there was one semi-surprise. My brother was listed as one of her survivors.

I had always been told that her family did not like Brother. It surprised that they did not remove his name before it was submitted for publication. I am not sure whose idea it was, but he was only listed as a friend. No mention was made of their marriage.

Her body was cremated and interred at her church, which always played an important part in her life.

The memorial service took place at the church the following month. I was the only one in our family who attended the memorial service. Brother refused to go.

The church was filled with family and friends. The service was beautiful. I am sure that it was exactly what XSIL wanted it to be. It was the perfect ending to a life well lived.

I noticed during the service that it was being recorded. There were several cameras being used. Even though Brother had chosen not to attend, I thought that he might enjoy watching a video of the service – whenever he felt comfortable doing so.

The day after the service, I called the church office and ask if I could purchase a copy of the video. To my surprise, the answer was a definite no. The video was only for the family, and former brother-in-law did not count as family.

Even though I was unable to obtain a copy of the video, I told Brother that I had called the church. His response surprised me, although looking back on it, I should have expected his reply. His actual words and his tone, though, said two different things.

His words were something like, "Why did you do that? I would never watch it."

His tone, though, was more like, "You stupid ignorant fool. Why the hell would you do something so stupid. I would never – EVER - watch that crap."

Nothing else was ever said about it.

A short time later, Brother told me that he had applied for and had been granted XSIL's Social Security Disability payments. I was shocked then, and I am still in shock over this.

He was not yet old enough to receive Social Security benefits on his own. He was not, and is not, disabled. He divorced this woman decades ago. And he murdered her. And now the government is sending him a monthly check. This is wrong on so many levels.

So, yes, I do believe with all my heart that my brother (I refer to him as my ex-brother) is evil, a psychopath, a sociopath, and an unrepentant serial killer.

What do you think?

It is highly unlikely that Brother will ever admit to killing his ex-wife and his mother. I am sure that he will lie about it until his dying day.

In 2017, Brother told me, by email, that he would never speak to me or have anything to do with me for the rest of our lives. He did this because he said that I insinuated that he lied about something (totally unrelated to murder).

Let me tell you about two of his lies. Brother has a favorite dating site.

AN UNNECESSARY END

He has met several women this way and has recommended the site to other people. Out of curiously, I looked at his profile one day. It was rather routine, no surprises, but he did say that he is a college graduate. He was a mediocre student for two years. I do not think the university considered that worthy of a diploma. He should not have lied about it, but I would guess that most people who use dating apps lie about one thing or another, or so I have heard,

But there is one instance of lying that still bothers me years later.

In his lifetime, Brother has run for public office on many occasions. Some were local elections, and some were statewide. He won some. He lost some.

One year, he ran for mayor of HomeTown and a statewide position at the same time. He lost both.

As is their custom, the largest newspaper in the state, with statewide coverage, reached out to each person running for a statewide position to supply biographical information to be published in the newspaper.

An Unnecessary End

For his marital status, Brother told them that he is a widower (referring to his first ex-wife, whom he murdered).

He replied that he has two daughters and one grandson. This is very much a lie. Brother has no children at all. That obviously means he has no grandchildren at all.

Why would someone lie about the very basics of his life, which many people would know were not true, if he wanted the people of our state to vote him into office?

I think his lies to the newspaper reveal so much about his true character.

I would never pretend to know what is going on in Brother's odd little mind. I am sure that I will never know his motive for killing his ex-wife. I do know, however, that whenever Brother finds a situation or a person to be inconvenient, he finds a way to remove it/him/her from his life, either temporarily or permanently.

Do you believe that Brother killed his mother and/or ex-wife? Let us know what you think.

Our cemeteries and mausoleums are filled with people who died due to the deliberate actions of a caretaker. If you have firsthand knowledge of a similar story, please share it with us.

Tullisian Books
"An Unnecessary End"
PO Box 3118
Little Rock AR 72203-3118

or

books@tullisian.com
Subject line: "An Unnecessary End"

"Never worry about who will be offended if you speak the truth. Worry about who will be misled, deceived, and destroyed if you don't."

-Unknown

"When I sit down to write a book, I do not say to myself, 'I am going to produce a work of art.' I write it because there is some lie that I want to expose, some fact to which I want to draw attention, and my initial concern is to get a hearing."

-George Orwell